What Happens When We Pray?

Bisi Oladipupo

Springs of life publishing

Copyright © 2023 by Bisi Oladipupo

Springs of life publishing

ISBN: 978-1-915269-33-1 (ePub e-book)

ISBN: (978-1-915269-32-4 (paperback)

All Rights Reserved.

No part of this book may be used or reproduced by any means, graphic, electronic, or mechanical, including photocopying, recording, taping, or by any information storage retrieval system without the written permission of the publisher except in the case of brief quotations embodied in critical articles and reviews.

Printed in the United Kingdom

Unless otherwise indicated, scripture quotations are taken from the New King James Version.

Scripture taken from the New King James Version®. Copyright © 1982 by Thomas Nelson. Used by permission. All rights reserved.

Scripture quotations from The Authorized (King James) Version. Rights in the Authorized Version in the United Kingdom are vested in the Crown. Reproduced by permission of the Crown's patentee, Cambridge University Press.

Scripture quotations marked (NLT) are taken from the Holy Bible, New Living Translation, copyright ©1996, 2004, 2015 by Tyndale House Foundation. Used by permission of Tyndale House Publishers, Carol Stream, Illinois 60188. All rights reserved.

Scripture quotations marked (AMP) are taken from the Amplified Bible, Copyright © 2015 by The Lockman Foundation. Used by permission.

Contents

Dedication	IV
Foreword	V
1. Introduction	1
2. What We Approach When We Pray	3
3. Response to Our Prayers	9
4. Our Position in the Place of Prayer	21
5. Different Types of Prayer	25
6. Hindrances to Prayer	36
7. How Long Should I Pray For?	40
8. Conclusion	43
Salvation Prayer	45
About the Author	46
Also By Bisi	47
Afterword	49

Dedication

To Jesus Christ my Lord and saviour; to Him alone that laid down His life that l might have life eternal. To Him that lead captivity captive and gave gifts unto men (Ephesians 4; 8). One of those gifts is writing!

Bisi Oladipupo

Foreword

The truth is, prayer meetings tend to be the least attended church services generally. In recent years, we have seen online global prayer movements, and we are grateful for this. However, the matter of prayer is still a struggle for many.

This kingdom works by faith. In other words, when we pray, we must see what is happening in the spiritual realm through the eyes of faith.

This book will look at what happens when we pray. Whatever position we are when we pray, know that much more is happening.

If only we could see with our eyes of faith what happens when we pray, prayer will become more enjoyable and a lifestyle.

My prayer is that you will have a different perspective on prayer after reading this book.

Enjoy!

Bisi

Chapter 1

Introduction

Did you know that when you pray, so much happens? We get up in the morning and pray; some go to dedicated places to pray, and others make prayer a lifestyle.

Whatever approach we have to prayer, so much happens when we pray. Our challenge in this physical world is that we do not see what happens in the spiritual realm. This is why we are told to live by faith (Romans 1:17) and to live and walk in the Spirit (Galatians 5:25). Hence, it is crucial to maintain a vibrant prayer life in addition to praying according to the will of God and praying effective prayers.

Did you know we take a position in the spirit when we pray? Did you know that when we pray, we approach a person, an actual throne, and much more happens?

This book will look at various things that happen when we pray. It will look at some examples in Scripture and the results of prayer.

The scriptures tell us that our "expectation shall not be cut off" (Proverbs 23:18; KJV). When we pray, we must go to God with great expectation.

Now, let us have a look at what happens when we pray.

Chapter 2
What We Approach When We Pray

We will now look at what we approach when we pray. Yes, we may kneel near our beds or pray with others in a church service, but much more is happening.

We Come Unto the Throne of Grace

The Scripture tells us that we come unto the throne of grace when we pray.

"**14** Seeing then that we have a great High Priest who has passed through the heavens, Jesus the Son of God, let us hold fast *our* confession. **15** For we do not have a High Priest who cannot sympathize with our weaknesses, but was in all *points* tempted as *we are, yet* without sin. ⁱ⁶ Let us therefore come boldly to the throne of grace, that we may obtain mercy and find grace to help in time of need" (Hebrews 4:14-16).

It is so important to imagine what happens when we pray. According to this scripture, we come to the throne of grace. We know that God's throne is a throne of grace.

However, have you ever pictured what that looks like? We have a few scriptures that tell us what the throne of God is.

"*² Immediately I was in the Spirit; and behold, a throne set in heaven, and One sat on the throne. ³ And He who sat there was like a jasper and a sardius stone in appearance; and there was a rainbow around the throne, in appearance like an emerald. ⁴ Around the throne were twenty-four thrones, and on the thrones I saw twenty-four elders sitting, clothed in white robes; and they had crowns of gold on their heads. ⁵ And from the throne proceeded lightnings, thunderings, and voices. Seven lamps of fire were burning before the throne, which are the[d] seven Spirits of God*" (Revelation 4:2-5).

When we pray, we are coming to the greatest throne that there can ever be. The one who sits upon the throne is called the ancient of days (Daniel 7:9).

"Your throne, O God, *is* forever and ever; A scepter of righteousness *is* the scepter of Your kingdom" (Psalm 45:6).

It will take revelation knowledge to imagine how the throne of God is, but this is what we come to when we pray. The Bible tells us in the Book of Hebrews that it is the throne of grace.

Therefore, when we pray, we come to a real throne in the spirit. This throne is real, and nothing can compare to it. We need to meditate on this. At His throne, we receive mercy and grace to help in times of need.

We Come Unto Mount Zion

Prayer is not just asking for things. Prayer is communication with our heavenly Father. Prayer is fellowship; it is also communion. Waiting on the Lord is also prayer.

In the Old Testament, the children of Israel were invited up to the mount, but they refused the invitation (Exodus 19:13; Deuteronomy 5:23-31). For the sake of emphasis, let us look at some parts of these scriptures:

"27 You go near and hear all that the Lord our God may say, and tell us all that the Lord our God says to you, and we will hear and do it.'

28 "Then the Lord heard the voice of your words when you spoke to me, and the Lord said to me: 'I have heard the voice of the words of this people which they have spoken to you. They are right in all that they have spoken. 29 Oh, that they had such a heart in them that they would fear Me and always keep all My commandments, that it might be well with them and with their children forever! 30 Go and say to them, "Return to your tents." 31 But as for you, stand here by Me, and I will speak to you all the commandments, the statutes, and the judgments which you shall teach them, that they may observe them in the land which I am giving them to possess'" (Deuteronomy 5:27-31).

We can see from the above scriptures that the children of Israel were invited up the mountain to hear the Lord speak.

In the Book of Hebrews, we are told that we have not come to a mountain that can be touched and that burns with fire (Hebrews 12:18–21). In the New Covenant, we have come to a spiritual mountain called Mount Zion. In the place of prayer and communion with God, we must see this with the eye of faith.

"22 But you have come to Mount Zion and to the city of the living God, the heavenly Jerusalem, to an innumerable company of angels, 23 to the [j]general assembly and church of the firstborn who are registered in heaven, to God the Judge of all, to the spirits of just men made perfect, 24 to Jesus the Mediator of the new covenant, and to the blood of sprinkling that speaks better things than that of Abel" (Hebrews 12:22-24).

From this scripture, we can further see what we have come to:

- Mount Zion
- The city of the living God
- The heavenly Jerusalem
- An innumerable company of angels
- The general assembly

- Church of the firstborn
- To God the Judge of all
- To the spirits of just men made perfect
- To Jesus the mediator of the New Covenant
- To the blood of sprinkling that speaks better things than that of Abel

This is simply amazing!

The Children of Israel saw a physical mountain that could be touched, but we have a spiritual mountain. This is a spiritual reality in communion with God.

We Come Unto the God of all Flesh

When we pray, we come unto the God of all flesh, of whom nothing is too hard for.

"Behold, I am the Lord, the God of all flesh. Is there anything too hard for Me? (Jeremiah 32:27).

O You who hear prayer, To You all flesh will come (Psalm 65:2).

In the place of prayer, we come to Him who can do all things. All we need to do is believe, for all things are possible to him who believes (Mark 9:23). God needs our faith, for he who comes to God must believe that He is and that He is a rewarder of those who diligently seek Him (Hebrews 11:6).

When we approach God our Father, we must come in faith. Faith is simply trusting our heavenly Father that loves us.

Chapter 3
Response to Our Prayers

Prayer is such a powerful thing. If only we knew what prayer does in the spiritual realm, our prayer meetings would be flooded with people. Nobody would be coerced to pray.

Did you know that our prayers are offered on the golden altar before the throne of God?

"²And I saw the seven angels who stand before God, and to them were given seven trumpets. ³ Then another angel, having a golden censer, came and stood at the altar. He was given much incense, **that he should offer it with the prayers of all the saints upon the golden altar which was before the throne.** *⁴ And the smoke of the incense,* **with the prayers of the saints, ascended before God from the angel's hand**" (Revelation 8:2-4).

This is very powerful; our prayers are actually presented on the golden altar before the throne of God.

We can also find where it is stated that our prayers are like fragrances (Revelation 5:8). We all know that incense and fragrance in the natural linger. Could this be the reason the Lord sent Peter to Cornelius—that his arms and prayers had come up as a memorial before God (Acts 10:4)? Our God does not forget our prayers. This is why the prayers of past generations are still working today.

Let us now have a look at the response to prayers.

We now know what we approach when we pray and what happens to our prayers. Let us now look at the response to our prayers.

The Bible tells us that God does not change (Malachi 3:6). What He did for one, He will do for another. We have amazing, documented answers to prayers in Scripture, and many of us have experienced the power of God in prayer. God is indeed a prayer-answering God. The foundation of a vibrant prayer life is knowing that God loves us and keeps covenant. God is for us, and our faith works through love (Galatians 5:6).

Prison Doors Opened

Paul and Silas were put into jail because Paul cast out a spirit of divination from a damsel and the hope her masters had in getting profits was gone (Acts 16:9-23).

When Paul and Silas got into prison, the Bible does not say that they complained, *"O God, you told us to come to Macedonia. See what has happened to us!"* No, the Scripture tells us that they prayed and sang praises to God.

Let us see the response to their prayers and praises:

*"**25** But at midnight Paul and Silas were praying and singing hymns to God, and the prisoners were listening to them. **26** Suddenly there was a great earthquake, so that the foundations of the prison were shaken; and immediately all the doors were opened and everyone's chains were loosed. **27** And the keeper of the prison, awaking from sleep and seeing the prison doors open, supposing the prisoners had fled, drew his sword and was about to kill himself. **28** But Paul called with a loud voice, saying, "Do yourself no harm, for we are all here"* (Acts 16:25-28).

Figuratively, prison doors still open, and chains fall off when we pray. The earthquake and foundations of the prison were shaken due to the prayer and praise of Paul and Silas.

Boldness Imparted by the Holy Spirit

Peter and John were threatened because they healed a man who had been lame from his mother's womb (Acts 4:22). They were told not to speak at all nor teach in the name of Jesus (Acts 4:18).

Subsequently, Peter and John went to their own company, reported what happened (Acts 4:23), and then prayed. Their prayer can be found in Acts 4:24-30. Let us look at the response to their prayer:

*"**31** And when they had prayed, the place where they were assembled together was shaken; and they were all filled with the Holy Spirit, and they spoke the word of God with boldness"* (Acts 4: 31).

This is another result of prayer—being filled with the Holy Spirit and having the ability to speak God's Word with boldness.

The Barren Gives Birth

An angel was sent to Zacharias to tell him that his prayers had been heard and that Elisabeth would have a child (Luke 1:11-13). Scripture tells us that both of them were old, well stricken in years, and Elisabeth was barren (Luke 1:7). The angel's visitation was in response to Zacharias' prayers, and they gave birth to John the Baptist (Luke 1:57).

The angelic visitation was in direct response to his prayers. Elisabeth and Zacharias gave birth to one called the greatest prophet born of woman (Luke 7:28).

Hannah is another woman whom God answered her prayers, and she gave birth to Samuel. The account can be found in the Book of 1 Samuel 1. Scripture tells us that none of Samuel's words fell to the ground (1 Samuel 3:19). In other words, all that he said by the Lord came to pass.

Life is Extended

We have an account in Scripture that tells us that Hezekiah was sick unto death. Then the Lord sent Prophet Isaiah to tell him to put his house in order (Isaiah 38:1). Hezekiah prayed, and the Lord not only healed him but also extended his life by fifteen years (Isaiah 38:4-5). Hezekiah's healing and extension of life were in direct response to his prayers. Remember that the initial word from the Lord was that he was going to die and that he should set his house in order.

Battles Are Won

We find many accounts in the Old Testament where they cried to the Lord and won battles. We have an account where Jehoshaphat prayed, proclaimed a fast and sought the face of God when the children of Moab, Ammon, and others came to battle against Jehoshaphat. The Lord answered his prayer, and he was given a word: *"For the battle is not yours but God's"* (2 Chronicles 20:15). God fought for Jehoshaphat, the people of Judah, and Jerusalem, and they won.

The Scripture says, *"And the fear of God was on all the kingdoms of those countries when they heard that the Lord had fought against the enemies of Israel. Then the realm of Jehoshaphat was quiet, for his God gave him rest all around"* (2 Chronicles 20:29-30).

Do you have something that is boasting against you? Why not take it to the Lord in prayer and let Him fight your battles for you?

Several years ago, I applied for a job that I was qualified for and had the necessary experience. In fact, I was actually doing a similar role when I applied for the job. Time went by, and I never heard from this organisation. So, I called and asked if I could get an update about the role I applied for. I was told that I was not shortlisted. I was amazed, as I was doing a similar role. I asked why I was not shortlisted, but no legitimate response was forthcoming.

Then I decided to write in and ask why I was not shortlisted, and I left it to the Lord.

One day at work, I received a telephone call from the organisation. The gentleman said that he was calling in response to my letter. He apologised and said my application was not shortlisted due to an oversight. He then said that although they had already interviewed ten people for the role, if I was still interested, I would be offered an interview. I said yes, and the rest is history. I was offered the job, and I worked there for five years.

This is a practical example of when God fights for us.

Women Receive Their dead Back to Life

In the Book of 2 Kings, we have an account of the Shunammite woman who refused to take no for an answer. She insisted on the man of God praying for her dead son. Elisha prayed and stretched himself on the child, and the child came back to life (2 Kings 4:17-36). In the Book of Hebrews, it is safe to say that what happened here is part of this scripture, *"Women received their dead back to life again"* (Hebrews 11:35).

Curses Are Turned Around

Abraham journeyed and went to Gerar. He introduced Sarah as his sister; therefore, Abimelech took her. Obviously, Abimelech did this innocently, as Abraham never said that Sarah was his wife. Nevertheless, this did not stop him from getting into trouble with God.

God told Abimelech in a dream that he was a dead man because he had taken a man's wife (Genesis 20:3). Abimelech then released Sarah back to Abraham.

The scriptures tell us that Abraham prayed to God and healed Abimelech, his wife, and his maidservants, and they bore children. Why was this necessary? Taking Abraham's wife had consequences.

"*17 So Abraham prayed to God; and God healed Abimelech, his wife, and his female servants. Then they bore children; 18 for the Lord had closed up all the wombs of the house of Abimelech because of Sarah, Abraham's wife*" (Genesis 20:17-18).

It took prayer for the wombs of all those in Abimelech's house to be opened.

We Are able to live a Peaceful Life

The believers in Christ in each land are responsible for praying for their country. The Bible instructs us to pray for our leaders. The scriptures also tell us the results of our prayer:

"Therefore I [a] exhort first of all that supplications, prayers, intercessions, and giving of thanks be made for all men, ² for kings and all who are in [b] authority, that we may lead a quiet and peaceable life in all godliness and [c] reverence. ³ For this is good and acceptable in the sight of God our Savior, ⁴ who desires all men to be saved and to come to the knowledge of the truth" (1 Timothy 2:1-4).

When we pray, it will make it easier to share the gospel. We have to pray for those in authority so that godly laws are introduced, bringing peace to our lands.

We Pray Mysteries in the Spirit

When we pray in the Spirit, our mind is unfruitful. This simply means that our minds are not taking part, but our spirit is speaking mysteries in the spirit.

"For he who speaks in a tongue does not speak to men but to God, for no one understands *him;* however, in the spirit he speaks mysteries" (1 Corinthians 14:2).

It takes faith to pray in the Spirit; however, praying in the Spirit has great rewards. There is only so much we will know about how to pray in our understanding, but the Spirit of God knows exactly what we should be praying about.

There have been many testimonies of people praying in the Spirit with outstanding results. The Bible also tells us that it is the Holy Spirit who is helping us to pray (Romans 8:26).

Many years ago, I was going to travel to visit my family in Africa. Knowing all the news and concerns in Africa, I took extra time to pray before the trip. It was fascinating that after a period of praying, I knew to the minute detail what to get for some specific family members that I would see without them making any requests. Simply amazing!

Divine Strength Is Received

The scriptures tell us that those who wait upon the Lord shall have their strength renewed (Isaiah 40:31). Waiting upon the Lord is an act that is also done at the place of prayer.

We have an account in the Bible where Samson tells a woman the secret of his strength. She betrayed him and told his secret to his enemies. That was the end of his supernatural strength (Judges 16:16-20).

At the hand of his enemies, Samson prayed for strength, and the Lord answered him.

*"²⁸ Then Samson called to the Lord, saying, "O Lord God, remember me, I pray! **Strengthen me, I pray, just this once,** O God, that I may with one blow take vengeance on the Philistines for my two eyes!" ²⁹ And Samson took hold of the two middle pillars which supported the temple, and he braced himself against them, one on his right and the other on his left. ³⁰ Then Samson said, "Let me die with the Philistines!" And he pushed with all his might, and the temple fell on the **lords and all the people who were in it. So the dead that he killed at his death were more than he had killed in his life**"* (Judges 16:28-30).

Samson would not have been able to do what he did without the strength of God, and this strength was in direct response to his prayer.

Wrong Counsels Are Turned Around

David was informed that Ahithophel was among the conspirators with Absalom. David then prayed and asked the Lord to turn Ahithophel's counsel into foolishness (2 Samuel 15:31). God answered David's prayer as Ahithophel's counsel was not followed (2 Samuel 16:23).

Does anyone have wrong counsel against you? Is anyone ganging up against you? This is a prayer that you could pray.

Mercy is Obtained From God

Scripture tells us that Ahab was a very wicked king. As a matter of fact, the Bible tells us that Ahab did evil in the sight of the Lord above all that were before him (1 Kings 16:30).

This simply tells us how wicked Ahab was. The Lord sent Elijah to tell him what would happen. Although Ahab was wicked, he humbled himself before the Lord. The Lord then sent Ahab a word that the evil would not be in his days but in the days of his son (1 Kings 21:29). Why did Ahab get mercy from God? Because he humbled himself.

"See how Ahab has humbled himself before Me? Because he has humbled himself before Me, I will not bring the calamity in his days. In the days of his son I will bring the calamity on his house" (1 Kings 21:29).

Our God delights in mercy (Micah 7:18).

Translated Into the Kingdom of Jesus Christ

The Bible tells us, "Whosoever calls upon the name of the Lord shall be saved" (Romans 10:13). This is the criteria for anyone who wants to come to the Lord. A simple prayer will bring a great and eternal change in anyone's life (Colossians 1:13).

Healing Received

Our prayers are effective; many have received healing from others praying for them. The Scripture tells us: "Confess *your* trespasses to one another, and pray for one another, that you may be healed..." (James 5:16).

Healing belongs to us, and sometimes the manifestation of that healing comes when we pray for one another.

Secrets Are Revealed in the Place of Prayer

Daniel and his friends would have been killed had they not known how to pray. The king had a dream and wanted someone to tell him the dream and its interpretation. Daniel and his friends prayed, and God revealed the dream to Daniel with its interpretation (Daniel 2).

We Are Built Up

When we pray in the Spirit, we are also building ourselves up:

"But you, beloved, building yourselves up on your most holy faith, praying in the Holy Spirit" (Jude 1:20).

There are many advantages to praying in the Spirit; one is building ourselves up.

Chapter 4

Our Position in the Place of Prayer

For us to have confidence in our place of prayer, we must know our position in the Spirit. We must be aware of what Jesus Christ our Lord has done for us and who we are now in Him.

If you had a good earthly father who loved you, would you not have confidence in approaching him and asking or making a demand? The scriptures tell us, "Beloved, now are we the sons of God" (1 John 3:2). We are children of God.

Let us look at various positions we can take in the place of prayer.

Child of God

It has been stated above that we are now children of God. What a privilege we have in Christ! The Scripture further tells us that if we, as earthly parents, can respond to our children, how much more our heavenly Father!

"9 Or what man is there among you who, if his son asks for bread, will give him a stone? 10 Or if he asks for a fish, will he give him a serpent? 11 If you then, being evil, know how to give good gifts to your children, how much more will your Father who is in heaven give good things to those who ask Him!" (Matthew 7:9-11).

In other words, earthly parents respond to the requests of their children and give them what they ask for. How much more our heavenly Father? We must have this confidence in the place of prayer.

Friend of God

The scriptures tell us that Abraham was called a friend of God (James 2:23).

Friends have access to information others do not (John 15:15).

The Lord revealed to Abraham that He was going to destroy Sodom and Gomorrah because of Abraham's relationship with the Lord (Genesis 18:17). Abraham was then able to intercede for the city (Genesis 18:23-33).

We all have an invitation to become friends with God.

"14 You are My friends if you do whatever I command you. 15 No longer do I call you servants, for a servant does not know what his master is doing; but I have called you friends, for all things that I heard from My Father I have made known to you" (John 15:14-15).

This is a place of intimacy with God. This is the relationship that Abraham had with the Lord.

Priests and Kings

Looking at the role of the priest in the Old Testament, we can see that priests stood in the gap for people. Phinehas stopped the plague that came to the children of Israel, which pleased the Lord (Numbers 25:6-12). During the earthly ministry of Jesus Christ our Lord, after healing a leper, the Lord told him to go and show himself unto the priest (Mark 1:44). Priests in the Bible offered sacrifices for the people.

Our Lord Jesus Christ is our high priest (Hebrews 2:17; 4:14).

The Scripture further tells us that high priests, on behalf of God for men, offer gifts and sacrifices for sin (Hebrews 5:1). Now that Jesus has paid the ultimate price for us (Hebrews 9:24-28), there is no need for that. However, we can learn from the office of a priest.

Priests stand in the gap for others, and this is what we do in the place of prayer.

We know that kings make decrees. Some parts of the world still have kings, and they can relate to this.

The scriptures tell us that we have been made kings and priests unto God (Revelation 1:6). So, we pray for others and make decrees in the spirit. God, our Father, backs us up because we are His kings and priests here on this earth.

The Bible further defines our position as priests and calls us a "royal priesthood" (1 Peter 2:9).

Therefore, in the place of prayer, we are not beggars. We are God's kings and priests, enforcing His kingdom down here on earth in the place of prayer.

We can see Moses taking his place, praying for others in the place of prayer. Moses stood in the gap for the children of Israel when they disobeyed the Lord (Exodus 32:11-14).

The scriptures also tell us that we are a royal priesthood (1 Peter 2:9). The title, "royal", stems from who we belong to. We are children of God in Christ; therefore, we are royals. We need to see ourselves for who we are in the place of prayer.

Chapter 5

Different Types of Prayer

In order to determine the different types of prayer, we will look at Scripture to see what it says about prayer.

In Scripture, we find different ways to pray. Before we go into that, it is safe to say that every prayer is a prayer of faith. What does this mean? It simply means we believe that God heard us. So, whatever our approach to prayer, we must always come to the Lord in faith.

Now, let us look at various types of prayer.

Asking, Seeking, and Knocking

In the Book of Matthew, we find this clearly stated:

"⁷ Ask, and it will be given to you; seek, and you will find; knock, and it will be opened to you. ⁸ For everyone who asks receives, and he who seeks finds, and to him who knocks it will be opened" (Matthew 7:7-8).

The word "ask" is very clear. We ask, and we receive. When we do ask, we must ask according to His will. In other words, what we are asking for must not be outside the will of God. It must be according to His revealed will.

"¹⁴ Now this is the confidence that we have in Him, that if we ask anything according to His will, He hears us. ¹⁵ And if we know that He hears us, whatever we ask, we know that we have the petitions that we have asked of Him" (1 John 5:14-15).

A good example of this would be asking God for a job. We know the Lord wants us to work and provide for the family (2 Thessalonians 3:10 & 1 Timothy 5:8).

There is a bit more to the prayer of seeking. Sometimes, we do not know what we ask for; therefore, we need to seek. If we don't know what direction to take on a matter, we would need to simply ask for direction and seek the answer. The answer can come in various ways. It could be a witness in our spirits, a prophetic word to confirm what we know in our spirits, or supernatural arrangements that make it very clear that this is the answer. In another instance, we can be given specific steps to take. Each step would eventually lead to what we sought.

The scriptures tell us that when we seek, we will find.

Knocking is another phase in prayer. In the natural, there are many reasons a person would knock on a door. Knocking is normally done to gain someone's attention or have access to something that is not currently available. The Bible tells us that when we knock, it will be opened to us.

Perhaps we could say that knocking is when a person knows what they want, but the door has not been opened yet. This can be used spiritually. If there is something that a person desires, then the technique of knocking will open the door.

The prayer of knocking is a persistent prayer. In the natural, if a person knocks on a door and gets no response, they will knock again until someone opens the door. The scriptures say that when we knock, it shall be opened.

We can see this type of prayer being expanded on by the Lord in the Book of Luke.

"5 And He said to them, "Which of you shall have a friend, and go to him at midnight and say to him, 'Friend, lend me three loaves; 6 for a friend of mine has come to me on his journey, and I have nothing to set before him'; 7 and he will answer from within and say, 'Do not trouble me; the door is now shut, and my children are with me in bed; I cannot rise and give to you'? 8 I say to you, though he will not rise and give to him because he is his friend, yet because of his persistence he will rise and give him as many as he needs.

Keep Asking, Seeking, Knocking

⁹ "So I say to you, ask, and it will be given to you; seek, and you will find; knock, and it will be opened to you. ¹⁰ For everyone who asks receives, and he who seeks finds, and to him who knocks it will be opened" (Luke 11:5-10).

When we look at the narrative the Lord used to teach in this verse, we find that this friend's door was already locked, and his children were in bed. However, the friend refused to knock once and say, *"Oh, he is sleeping and in bed now"*. This person must have kept knocking until the door was opened. Verse eight of the above scripture confirms this.

Sometimes, we have to be persistent in prayer to get results.

Prayer of Giving Thanks

Sometimes, when we hear the word "giving of thanks", for some reason, we tend not to attach it to prayer. However, did you know that "giving of thanks" gets a response from the Lord just as we would expect an answer from a petition prayer?

In the Book of Philippians, we can see this very clearly:

"⁶ Be anxious for nothing, but in everything by prayer and supplication, with thanksgiving, let your requests be made known to God; ⁷ and the peace of God, which surpasses all understanding, will guard your hearts and minds through Christ Jesus" (Philippians 4:6-7).

WHAT HAPPENS WHEN WE PRAY?

If you look at the above verse, the scripture tells us that with "prayer and supplication with thanksgiving", our requests should be made known to God. Therefore, thanksgiving is actually a prayer that gets a response.

We can see further examples of this in Scripture. When the leper came to thank Jesus after he was healed, he was simply thanking God. Jesus told him that his faith had made him whole (Luke 17:19). This leper was made whole because he gave thanks. He was not looking to be whole; he was just grateful that he was healed (Luke 17:15). Thanksgiving caused him to be whole without asking for it.

Scripture tells us to pray for all men and those in authority. Again, we can see that thanksgiving is actually a prayer:

"*Therefore I [a] exhort first of all that supplications, prayers, intercessions,* ***and giving of thanks be made for all men,*** *² for kings and all who are in [b] authority,* ***that we may lead a quiet and peaceable life in all godliness and*** *[c]* ***reverence.*** *³ For this is good and acceptable in the sight of God our Savior*" (1 Timothy 2:1-3).

Continue in prayer, and watch in the same with thanksgiving (Colossians 4:2; KJV).

Looking at some of the prayers of our Lord Jesus Christ during His earthly ministry, our Lord prayed thanksgiving prayers. At the last supper, Jesus gave thanks (1 Corinthians 11:24) and at the raising of Lazarus from the dead (John 11:41).

Speaking to the Situation

Speaking to the situation is also a type of prayer. When we look at the prayers our Lord Jesus Christ made when praying about sickness and the prayers of the disciples, they spoke to the situation.

"^{38} *Now He arose from the synagogue and entered Simon's house. But Simon's wife's mother was* [o]*sick with a high fever, and they made request of Him concerning her.* ^{39} *So He stood over her and rebuked the fever, and it left her. And immediately she arose and served them"* (Luke 4:38-39).

"Now Peter and John went up together to the temple at the hour of prayer, the ninth hour. ^{2} *And a certain man lame from his mother's womb was carried, whom they laid daily at the gate of the temple which is called Beautiful, to* [a]*ask alms from those who entered the temple;* ^{3} *who, seeing Peter and John about to go into the temple, asked for alms.* ^{4} *And fixing his eyes on him, with John, Peter said, "Look at us."* ^{5} *So he gave them his attention, expecting to receive something from them.* ^{6} *Then Peter said, "Silver and gold I do not have, but what I do have I give you: In the name of Jesus Christ of Nazareth, rise up and walk"* (Acts 3:1-6).

Our Lord Jesus Christ also spoke to the storm.

"^{35} *On the same day, when evening had come, He said to them, "Let us cross over to the other side."* ^{36} *Now when they had left the multitude, they took Him along in the boat as He was. And other little boats were also with Him.* ^{37} *And a great windstorm arose, and the waves beat into*

the boat, so that it was already filling. ³⁸ But He was in the stern, asleep on a pillow. And they awoke Him and said to Him, "Teacher, do You not care that we are perishing?"

³⁹ Then He arose and rebuked the wind, and said to the sea, "Peace,[] be still!" And the wind ceased and there was a great calm" (Mark 4:35-39).

Could it be that we are praying about situations that we need to speak to?

Jesus had spoken to a fig tree that had dried up from the root. Peter then told Jesus that the fig tree He had cursed had withered away (Mark 11:21). Our Lord Jesus Christ then said the following:

"²² So Jesus answered and said to them, "Have faith in God. ²³ For assuredly, I say to you, whoever says to this mountain, 'Be removed and be cast into the sea,' and does not doubt in his heart, but believes that those things he says will be done, he will have whatever he says. ²⁴ Therefore I say to you, whatever things you ask when you pray, believe that you receive them, and you will have them" (Mark 11:22-24).

Speaking to situations and making demands in Jesus' name is a form of prayer. Looking at verse twenty-four of the above, the statement starts with "therefore". This shows that the following action is specifically making a demand or speaking to a situation in prayer.

Every prayer we pray is a prayer of faith. It simply means that when we pray, we must believe that we will receive, and we shall have it.

Prayer of Intercession

The prayer of intercession is standing in the gap for someone. In the Old Testament, we see the Lord looking for a man:

"And I sought for a man among them, that should make up the hedge, and stand in the gap before me for the land, that I should not destroy it: but I found none" (Ezekiel 22:30).

In the Book of Timothy, we are also instructed to make intercession for all men and those in authority (1 Timothy 2:1-3).

As believers in Christ, we also have the Holy Spirit who makes intercession for the saints. We just need to learn how to yield in prayer and allow the Holy Spirit to pray through us.

"26 Likewise the Spirit also helps in our weaknesses. For we do not know what we should pray for as we ought, but the Spirit Himself makes intercession [a] for us with groanings which cannot be uttered. 27 Now He who searches the hearts knows what the mind of the Spirit is, because He makes intercession for the saints according to the will of God" (Romans 8:26-27).

Prayer of Consecration

Before our Lord Jesus Christ paid the ultimate sacrifice for all of us, He went to Mount Olives with His disciples (Luke 22:39). Jesus then prayed a prayer we could call the prayer of consecration. It is simply when we lay down our will for the Father's will. Sometimes, this is not easy, as we see Jesus Christ our Lord having to decide to follow what is written in His books (Hebrews 10:7).

*"**41** He walked away, about a stone's throw, and knelt down and prayed, **42** "Father, if you are willing, please take this cup of suffering away from me. Yet I want your will to be done, not mine." **43** Then an angel from heaven appeared and strengthened him. **44** He prayed more fervently, and he was in such agony of spirit that his sweat fell to the ground like great drops of blood.* (Luke 22:41-44; NLT).

Praying in the Spirit

When we pray in the Spirit, it is our spirit that is praying (1 Corinthians 14:14). We are told to always pray in the Spirit.

Pray in the Spirit at all times and on every occasion. Stay alert and be persistent in your prayers for all believers everywhere (Ephesians 6:18; NLT).

Paul is speaking here:

"I thank God that I speak in tongues more than any of you" (1 Corinthians 14:18; NLT).

The Scripture tells us that when we speak in tongues, we speak to God and speak mysteries (1 Corinthians 14:2).

There is only so much our natural understanding can take in prayer. We need to take advantage of this leverage in the Spirit.

Sometimes, the Lord will lay burdens on our hearts to pray. We need to yield to the person of the Holy Spirit and pray. We have no idea who is depending on our prayers.

The Lord needs us to cooperate with the person of the Holy Spirit to pray and establish the will of God here on earth.

The scriptures tell us that the Holy Spirit helps us pray. Notice the word "help". The Lord needs our cooperation so the Holy Spirit can help us in prayer.

^{26} Likewise the Spirit also helps in our weaknesses. For we do not know what we should pray for as we ought, but the Spirit Himself makes intercession [g]for us with groanings which cannot be uttered. ^{27} Now He who searches the hearts knows what the mind of the Spirit is, because He makes intercession for the saints according to the will of God (Romans 8:26-27).

Having looked at different types of prayer, we will briefly mention the weapons we have in the place of prayer:

The Name of Jesus

"If you ask anything in My name, I will do it" (John 14:14).

The Word of God

Put me in remembrance: let us plead together: declare thou, that thou mayest be justified (Isaiah 43:26; KJV).

The Blood of Jesus

"And to Jesus the Mediator of the new covenant, and to the blood of sprinkling that speaks better things than *that of* Abel (Hebrews 12:24; KJV).

Chapter 6

Hindrances to Prayer

Now that we know what happens in the place of prayer, the privileges we derive from prayer, and the different types of prayer, let us look at hindrances to prayer.

The things of the Kingdom of God operate through laws and principles. God's Word is called a law (Psalm 1:2; Psalm 119:72; James 1:25); therefore, it must be obeyed and followed. Let us now look at some hindrances to prayer.

Praying Amiss

Asking amiss means asking with the wrong motives or reasons.

3 You ask [God for something] and do not receive it, because you ask [d]with wrong motives [out of selfishness or with an unrighteous agen-

da], so that [when you get what you want] you may spend it on your [hedonistic] desires (James 4:3; AMP).

And even when you ask, you don't get it because your motives are all wrong—you want only what will give you pleasure (James 4:3; NLT).

Praying Unscriptural Prayers

We should only pray scriptural prayers that reflect the mind of God and are according to His will. If a person prayed for a married woman to become his wife, we know that such prayers would not be answered.

And this is the confidence we have in him: **if we ask any thing according to his will, he heareth us: (1 John 5:14; KJV).**

Conflict in Marriage

The Book of First Peter warns husbands that their prayers can be hindered if they do not honour their wives.

"Husbands, likewise, dwell with *them* with understanding, giving honor to the wife, as to the weaker vessel, and as *being* heirs together of the grace of life, that your prayers may not be hindered" (1 Peter 3:7).

Unforgiveness

The scriptures imply that unforgiveness can hinder our prayers. At the end of some verses where the Lord was talking about prayer, the Lord warned us about unforgiveness:

The Lesson of the Withered Fig Tree

[20] Now in the morning, as they passed by, they saw the fig tree dried up from the roots. [21] And Peter, remembering, said to Him, "Rabbi, look! The fig tree which You cursed has withered away."

[22] So Jesus answered and said to them, "Have faith in God. [23] For assuredly, I say to you, whoever says to this mountain, 'Be removed and be cast into the sea,' and does not doubt in his heart, but believes that those things he says will be done, he will have whatever he says. [24] Therefore I say to you, whatever things you ask when you pray, believe that you receive them, and you will have them.

Forgiveness and Prayer

[25] "And whenever you stand praying, if you have anything against anyone, forgive him, that your Father in heaven may also forgive you your trespasses. [26] But if you do not forgive, neither will your Father in heaven forgive your trespasses" (Mark 11:20-26).

We can see from the above scripture that the warning about unforgiveness is given directly after Jesus taught about prayer.

Therefore, our heavenly Father will not forgive us our trespasses if we do not forgive others. As a result, this will likely affect the prayer we pray.

Chapter 7

How Long Should I Pray For?

When we come to pray, the most important thing is to pray "effective prayers" (James 5:16).

Effective prayers can be short, long, or just a word.

When we look at scripture, there are examples of many short prayers that were very effective.

Samson:

"Then Samson called to the Lord, saying, "O Lord God, remember me, I pray! Strengthen me, I pray, just this once, O God, that I may with one blow take vengeance on the Philistines for my two eyes!" (Judges 16:28)

The Lord answered that prayer, and Samson killed more people after that prayer at his death than in his lifetime (Judges 16:30).

WHAT HAPPENS WHEN WE PRAY?

David:

"Then someone told David, saying, "Ahithophel is among the conspirators with Absalom." And David said, "O Lord, I pray, turn the counsel of Ahithophel into foolishness!" (2 Samuel 15:31).

The Lord did answer that prayer (2 Samuel 17:23).

And on the other hand, we have people like Elijah who prayed fervently. While we don't know how long Elijah prayed for, it appears it was not a short prayer (1 Kings 18:42-44 & James 5:17).

Jesus Christ, our Lord, prayed short prayers. Raising Lazarus from the dead was a short prayer (John 11:41-43), and Jesus Christ, our Lord, also prayed all night long (Luke 6:12). Jesus also asked His disciples why they could not pray with Him for one hour (Matthew 26:40).

The most important thing is that we pray Bible-based, effective prayers. Our prayers will have more impact as we grow in the knowledge of God and His word.

Our prayer lives need to grow.

The Bible tells us to "pray at all times" (1 Thessalonians 5:17) and pray in the Spirit always (Ephesians 6:18).

We must be prayerful people. Jesus Christ called His house "a house of prayer" (Matthew 21:13).

We can see from Scripture that we are to be people of prayer. How long an individual prays for is really down to the person. We must yield and obey whatever personal instructions the Lord gives us regarding our prayer life, and we should always yield to the Holy Spirit in the place of prayer.

Chapter 8

Conclusion

If only we knew how powerful our prayers were, our church prayer meetings would be much better attended.

The Lord needs our prayers to work on the earth and accomplish His desires. Could this be why we see Anna, the prophetess in the New Testament, dedicated to prayer?

"36 Now there was one, Anna, a prophetess, the daughter of Phanuel, of the tribe of Asher. She was of a great age, and had lived with a husband seven years from her virginity; 37 **and this woman was a widow [] of about eighty-four years, who did not depart from the temple, but served God with fastings and prayers night and day"** (Luke 2:36-37).

If those under the Old Testament received amazing results in the place of prayer, how much more we who are under a better covenant?

Let us return to the place of prayer and be expectant when we pray.

BISI OLADIPUPO

The Lord will do exceedingly abundantly above all we can ask or think (Ephesians 3:20).

What a privilege it is to pray!

Salvation Prayer

Father God, I come to you in Jesus' name. I admit that I am a sinner, and I now receive the sacrifice that Jesus Christ paid for me.

I confess with my mouth the Lord Jesus, and I believe in my heart that God raised Him from the dead.

I now declare that Jesus Christ is my Lord and Saviour.

Thank you, Father, for saving me in Jesus' name.

I am now your child. Amen.

If you've said this prayer for the first time, send an email to Bisiwriter@gmail.com .

Start reading your Bible and ask the Lord to guide you to a good church.

About the Author

Bisi Oladipupo is based in the United Kingdom with her family.

She has attended a few Bible colleges and has obtained a diploma in Biblical Studies from the UK and an associated degree in Bible and Theology from a USA school of ministry.

Her author page is www.bisiwriter.com, and her blog website is www.inspiredeords.org.

Also By Bisi

1. The Twelve Apostles of Jesus Christ: Lessons We Can Learn

2. The Lord's Cup in Communion: The Significance of taking the Lord's Supper

3. Different Ways to Receive Healing from Scripture and Walk in Health

4. Believing on The Name of Jesus Christ: What Every Believer Needs to Know

5. The Mind and Your Christian Walk: The Impact of the mind on our Christian walk

6. Relationship Skills in the Bible: Scriptural Principles of relating to others

7. The Nature of God's Kingdom: The Characteristics of the Kingdom of God

8. The Person of the Holy Spirit

9. 41 Insights from the Book of Revelation

10. The Importance of Spiritual Discernment

11. God Speaks Through Nature

12. It's All About the Heart

13. A Better Covenant: A Look at the Covenants of God and Our Better Covenant

14. 40 Day New Covenant Devotional

Afterword

If you enjoyed this book, please take a few moments to write a review of it online at the store where it was purchased. Thank you